Naming the Afternoon

p o e m s

Naming the Afternoon

Julia Johnson

Louisiana State University Press ❧ *Baton Rouge* 2002

Cloth
5 4 3 2 1
11 10 09 08 07 06 05 04 03 02

Paper
5 4 3 2 1
11 10 09 08 07 06 05 04 03 02

Designer: Amanda McDonald Scallan
Typeface: Adobe Caslon
Printer and binder: Thomson-Shore, Inc.

ISBN 0-8071-2810-4 (cloth)
ISBN 0-8071-2811-2 (paper)

The author gratefully acknowledges the editors of the following journals, in which some of these poems have appeared, sometimes in slightly different forms: *The Hollins Critic:* "An Example"; *Third Coast:* "Vernal Equinox": *64:* "The Rabbits," "Still Life with Woman," "The Way to Spell a Word," "The Drive"; *New Virginia Review:* "Revisiting Saint Louis Cemetery"; *Ascent:* "Leaving"; *Oxford Magazine:* "On the Contrary"; *Maple Leaf Rag:* "This Charm's Wound Up"; *New Orleans Review:* "Naming the Afternoon"; *The New Delta Review:* "The Kitchen of the Sleepless"; *20 Pounds of Headlights:* "The Bowl," "The Grand Table"; *Apostrophe:* "Fission"; *Poetry International:* "Two Children Are Threatened by a Nightingale"; *Eclipse:* "This Winter"; *Folio:* "Leaving Iowa."

"Memoir of a Woman of Pleasure" was originally published in *Elvis in Oz: New Stories and Poems from the Hollins College Creative Writing Program* (Charlottesville: University Press of Virginia, 1992).

For my parents

Contents

III

I

An Example

The sun is an example.
For what—a smooth dial, an elegant head?
The example before us, the circle
circling the house all day.
An example for an incandescent body of gases,
the planets revolving around.

The star nearest the earth.
Something like the sun, a light
fixed inside a keyhole: a room, a window, a tiny lake.

We watch it on our sheet of paper, its white self
passing, darkening through a pin's hole,
satisfied with its movement.
The earth's shadow erases it on the page.

We leave the exceeding brightness
of the early sun, concede how dark we have become,
our element of cold and winter's air left alone.
We are all the seven sleepers of Ephesus,
waking when light spreads through the dark
after two hundred years
and the trees lean into and cover the wide space.

Vernal Equinox

March 20. The equinox caught me
through the curtain this morning,
light weighing on the shelf, but invisible
in all the space of the room.
The sun crosses the equator, a line
I imagine to be sharp as the drawn line
of a map. Night and day grow equal everywhere
and hours end at the certainty of speed.
Everything else seems unexplained:
An egg sitting upright, unshaken,
as if with sudden life, on a table's metal top.
A wind which leaves the grass blades bent and leaning.
A double knock at the door.
I draw the hard pencil in one direction.
Things make a way to pair—
ring to horseshoe, hand in glove, shadow over light.

Deep Oceans

Below the mesopelagic realm, where daylight
weakens and fails, fish are gray
as walls. Something to do with equilibrium—
ocean with moon or without moon.
Something to do with depth regions, the darker
the ocean or the continental slope
and the shelf, rise, abyssal plain.
The division of ocean, split
into sections like the drawers of a chest.

I see this diagram, the size of my hand.
The deep oceans from the summer
in Gulf Shores, when I floated until beach swallowed the house
I watched from my raft. With each slope lower, meters
increase until finally, the last, a trench.
From the land, a slick plate, my mother sees me, a pale
blue square appearing and reappearing
only in the reflection of her glasses.

The phenomena of motion—the daily and half-daily tides
of the ocean. The deep blue of deep oceans, colors no one
can measure. It is all there for the eye, the green, polar
and coastal waters, blue the desert color of the sea.
Deep of oceans, deepest of them, where they are deep,
the steep incline from land to depth inward,
form the surface, maybe a serious thought, or a deep
sleep, the unknown time, the stories of a building,
windows clean eyes of its front face, the rooms, floors,
an imaginary space.

This chest is wooden and polished—
four drawers. A top as wide as one can see,

the knobs rattle. Inside each drawer, another chest
and inside it, again another. The sea inside a sea,
the sea floor above it, another sea floor spreading balance
and with the absence of wind, an anticlockwise spin,
a calm that only waits.

Nags Head in March

What light now brings shape
to these parts, mysteries left
displayed there; small angels drift
across waters' lid.

Huge dunes, huge sky, moon
a pearly dime, new icon
for what we can remember,
words for directions.

We mumble in wind,
yank at what topic we can.
A hang glider descends low
over the sand ridge.

Way out, way out, there
in dark blue haze, shadow caught
from edges, composition
sudden as some dreams.

On the other side,
the bay, brindled by loose waves
and calmer, pulls the sun in—
a smooth, yellow brim.

We walk this pale strip;
water surrounds all we know,
indeterminable now
as air, no measure.

The Rabbits

I have a habit of losing rabbits in my sleep.
They hop out, leave their baskets behind,
following me in the distance with their thick, ragged fur.
They are leading each other in a row
like a string of pearls lining the hill.
But I will lose them. The night will grow gray
in their eyes, like heavy sheep in heavy dirt.
I hug my last rabbit.

O from the road's rocky curb,
I am the marrow of a rabbit.
I will wait for them, turn over, count.
These rabbits will soon beg for me back, backing up the hill,
white blur across a tilted screen.

No News from Mount Sinai

No news from the collapse.
No news from the table of steadiness.
No news about the simplicity of the question.
No news about the lines of the hand,
a line that runs across the pine plank
or instructions on how to wind a watch,
instructions on or examples of how
to be afraid, no news on how to form a description,
how to draw an ox, how to create a notch in an edge.
No news from the paper concerning the cat.
No news on the noumenon;
the notice on the door must have fallen.
No news on the leggy girl who disappeared
from the corner yesterday.
No news on a change, a final change, or imitation,
separation, explanation.
No news on the repairing of the distrustful eye.

The Paragraph of Noon

October threads its difficult yarn, caught
in the hard edge, the edge in sequence against
the fan of lights' protracting wave,
and we too come, undone in light of the fact.
A light too soon heard, not seen.
How does the hand inside the hand not disappear?
As quiet as this, as quiet as the last step
from an empty hall. A woman stands listening
in the dark. We have come here, like strangers,
reversible faces lit by solitude's heat. Full-sprung
and heavy, the wake fails to repeat itself.
In fall, when the leaves turn yellow of yellow,
there must be nothing, nothing by which to recognize
noon's hold on the tide, the signed signature on the sand.
The crabs lose their busy race, like thoughts, here and there,
somewhat soon, noon takes the steep steps, and the horizon,
a tiny blue lasso, streams across the view.

Memoir of a Woman of Pleasure

These clocks, handy clocks. Six,
and the last finger slipped
slightly from my eye edge. Insight
I don't even know. The measure
to this certain pleasure I took
like an alleyway or rusted train
over swollen creeks, and he,
with a stomach of ball bearings,
a rope with becket around his neck;
we wore the same crown.
Five, the clocks wound tight,
their rickety bones,
pointed sharp pin-needles.
The clock, face on face, pleasured
woman in the face of each.
Four, chimes fell like steel throats,
and he was bound. At three, the birds
fiddled with their wiry heads,
and the minute, thrown like a discus,
split down our hands
before the last gesture.

On What We See

In these that spot the small evergreens,
reflect in the puddle beneath the roots, we
walk with the light.
I'm heavy on the ridge, the stars in the basket,
their breath in this new rhythm that touches
the hard box and what's left of the snow.
I have none in the loose pins, none in the horn's lasting sound.
Rain's spinning odd on the onset of spring.

Revisiting Saint Louis Cemetery

For the first time in the summer,
the wind melts a stillness between the trees.
We too know the unseen that these shadowed
mossy blocks bring. For whatever trust
there had been, a new set of news comes
telling through. You can almost see the cars now,
faint blurs of gray passing beyond sharp edges.
It is what you imagine when you come to these places:
a line of crabgrass taking a twist up the side of step,
a stone angel smiling beneath an oak's branch, her finger
curved and pointing. A horn blows from Basin Street.
Daylight, it must be true, ends later within these cracked
walls. From the outside, the curious crowds, wearing dresses
and suits, look in. For us, there are things that connect
and we take those with us. Darkness outspreads itself,
an even cloth under which we lie. How soon do those among us
leave? The blue ribbon tied to the wrought-iron gate loosens.
A woman steps out from a wide path, holding a bouquet,
and walks to the entrance.

for Larry Levis

The Hand Rests

The hand uncovers what is true,
a blade soft as water, a moving stone,
a play of opposites that leaves us
guessing but guides us to the gates
we know are locked.
At noon, at the perfect stroke,
the clock hands held together,
the air is hard. Everyone is walking
through without trouble, ghostly figures disappearing
within frames. What other opposites find us
at the most unexplained moment?
A face that doesn't please.
An objective without movement.
Leaving the house without feeling the ground.
Snow falling along an axis.
Noon waits for one minute
until it is gone, counting backward,
erasing itself.

Yellow

Yellow grass of all, yellow without
these hands, mine, soul yellow, the cup's
yellow lid. The yellow of hearts, and this seems
to be truest. Yellow is missing and blown.
This yellow bore no blooms. But yellow is strictest
way out there, like a triangle sail,
or the sun's dusk figure. Loosest is the yellow
of the light that follows.

The Locksmiths

This blue heat that wraps us,
sudden as a flag. We count the uncountable
in a remarkable flash. I have never understood
their unearthly light on the streets at night,
the cat's open yawn, asleep in her black cabinet.
The scales go home to their wedding tunes.
I have no room, no toes, no ears, a hidden
chest as full as the moon, a ripe stomach, and a kettle
that whispers throughout the morning and the night.
You've left me, the flowers broken at the stems, like a frog's
stiff jump. I'll tell you when the grounds shift, one more
ticket. For now the locks haven't mirrored themselves;
the stones are still the unthinkable. My head holds itself,
leaves me standing there.

The Earth Is a Trembling Man

He sees now the scale at which other things follow.
He is right as the tide on the clock.
He hurries without reason down corridors.
He burns glass on the shrill.
He steadies at night against the cool gray.
He breaks.
He is waiting for summer's recourse, senses divided.
He knows this image.
He fills the whole breadth of this broad channel.
He hangs above the line.
He discourages change like the edge of land.
He waits for the spoon to break, to fill
and tip to its next wobbly pose.

They Unfold the World

A napkin, then a tight square, eight
squares inside. Inside the house, they let
it open, unfold between their hands, hang
over their arms. The water runs out. The grass,
blades small as lace edge. They are feeling sick,
their stomachs grow large as buckets.
The world falls out of their hands, onto the tiles.
Outside on the porch, wind chimes crack.
"The world is only a sheet," one says.
"It is blue and open as the sea."
They slip off their shoes, lie down, and sleep
until there is no room to turn over.

In an Instant of Light

The light stands beneath the saddest pair, forever
a bewildered table of white.
They are the two fingers of the piano teacher's certain,
nimble hand. The blind eyes search the inside of a lid
for a truth, red or blue. Candles slip
into the wedding cake until the floor.
An image enters in, the clear arrow-shaped
wings of a slender bird. Wherever empty space,
two squares like front teeth, they pull
open. The moon lends itself only alone.
In five-minute intervals, the fly's white eyes bear
down on the plate and reflect.

Immortality

I have little room even to sit on this rooftop,
little room for my little leg. I keep secure, though,
my nervous white rabbit. Here, in the late morning,
no sun except for what it leaves on the trees,
the faint light like sugar specks. Each time I move,
I think the bird moves, mimicking me
because I'm some doll.
I like this most when the wind stops,
no chill anymore, and the table doesn't slide
against my spine in a push.
I'm listening hard to conversation:
love, weather, laughter, then the quiet
of nothing said, worrying me, so I look
at the ridiculous cat.
They must be family, too. I'm telling all this
to my rabbit. Listen. Is this really eternity?
Without a picture plane? I ask myself and the rabbit.
No answer. Sometimes my father tells me to eat my fish.
Sometimes my father tells me we have to get down from here.
The windows' black eyes are a black I've never seen.
This is a situation, I have a feeling, that will not change,
a still; we're permanent fixtures for some game.
No, too easy. We're really here, growing old.
It's something sudden scaring me, not the bird, the cat,
or the rabbit.
It's change in gravity, solemnity, or terrestrial gravitation.
In this sphere, we're drawing clumsy toward the center
of the earth. Everything is flat.
Where is it (or is it here), that place once beautiful?
That place still stored like a locket in my head,
where the people look around. My rabbit wants to jump
in the dark without being seen.
But I'm holding him with a grip I've just discovered.
My brother whispers into my head
what he says is a guess-who joke.
I am trying to hold onto my tongue and, crooked,
I find how easiest to sit.
The green around me stirs, but I have lost my restlessness—
my rabbit's fur is all that is felt.

Leaving

The blue sky has come into the room.
We close our windows to keep it in.
Our voices become whispers and finally,
like the silence, we too are invisible.

Rain outside on the grass, dust in the corner.
Every part of the sky is hard as stone, polished,
pushing the room in all directions.

We move between the points—
all that is left of the room's light,
of the sky's ether, of sense, of imagining
the strength at the center, of a final gesture,
a foregone truth, slowly leaving.

II

In the Evening Hour

Without worry, there is no need.
The pen on the paper splits
like any odd remembrance, jotted,
scarcely a letter formed, the words,
tiny emblems set free on the glass; we hum
in the silent dark, a face too soon forgotten
to describe. Which place? Which adjective?
A metaphorical breath, and you breathe
but do not utter what, a dove tail
spins from your lip, easy, unpredictable.
In this hour of the mood, the ending
comes and goes, a hand passing slowly across the wall.

Two Shovels, Crossed

You have the look of worry.
The wallboards overlap, and near the corner
a wide space throws shadows toward the wheelbarrow.
Your hands fan out like the awkward figures of birds.
You hold on to the black air,
and the only light left
in the shed, a sliver of simplest white.
Whose dirt rests on your scoop?
You've forgotten what it was like to reach
for the water hidden under the cold
and motionless cheek of her.

After the Flood

There was a likeness of you everywhere. The parlors overflowed
with mannequins, peach limbs spreading through doorways.
Outside, the sign above the All Right Insurance Company
hung by a loose hook. Breakables were locked in closets. I
floated toward the center, where there was equilibrium. I won-
dered what you looked like before all of this—how your hair
was tied, what sort of flowers were drawn on your dress, and
where you might have been lifted from, what position the waters swept you in, one arm above the head, a glass still held in
your hand. In the street, a girl's head was turning slowly down
into the manhole. Muted organ tones played from the radio in
the bathroom. A parade of people went by on their backs, their
hips and legs underwater, as if truncated by the sharp, gray surface. I found dryness in the hollow of a large can. I imagined
myself at sea, sleeping in a ship's hold, the tide pushing against
the side, rolling me on.

There Is That Noise

Not the one you hear now, the shuffling
of shoes inside your pillbox, the wind
behind the door. There is that noise
of a question, a noise rising higher and higher.
That noise of your own swallow or the shallow
hum of the heater. That noise that you think
you hear, no, know, a whisper tight and small
as a tooth. The noise of something spread, out,
over. A noise as you leave one room and enter
another. The rubbing, measuring, clap. The dark,
smooth shake of a man's laugh. No one is there.
Only a book closed tight in the corner of the hall.
There is that noise of the plate, stamping, tick,
changing of light. The noise of a pause.
The noise of no noise, the noise you hear
only when you are standing still.

On the Contrary

In these hours we can tell
what stillness holds us here,
what makes us shiver in our white shirts
like the simplest movement of the wind.

The darkest sky has ridden in; the man
at the door has stopped his knocking.
We leaf through our prayer books. In odd fashion,
the dappled damp ground sinks beneath us. Our boots
disappear. With each single breath we move closer,

like the waves, to what brought us:
light at the edges of our eyes, the cracking of rain.

We limp in our thoughts, the eraser works along
until there is nothing,
only a solid white egg, shifting
in the tide.

Naming the Afternoon

The girls without memory
are losing track of their steps,
eyes heavy as sacks.
They walk past the chapel,
the beds of small flowers.
At the edge of a pond, dirt glitters like salt.
They make their way over wet stones,
talking in rhyme, staying
within the trees' broken veil.

They reach the deserts and the sea.
Where are their sentences?
They borrow signatures and write them down—
the paths of crabs, traced by a little light.

The Charm's Wound Up

Finished the winding, the power complete,
a bottle closed tight or sealed lips
like two sharp knives, when everything is done,
a closed book, a look of solace, a latched door,
the gesture of motioning, come here, a wink,
to fascinate, the charming laugh, we place
hats on our heads, pull back down our skirts,
there is nothing left, no smile, three blurred
witches, white wind or the kettle on the stove,
the hand on the banister, a magician's empty
hat, the blossom without its bole or the sun
without its setting, the clock so tight
it will not move, a darkened lamp, the quiet
after a bullet's sound, a final toast,
the stationary ball in the grass, too spun,
too much, too used, the mouth too full with words.

The Shape of Losing

I have hung too little on the rack,
a taste for something old
and nothing new left off.

A handshake, a paper covering rock.
You have listed what has harmed you.
Now the next bell, the next play,
a riff of what waits.
If there is no score, no spin,
no deck of cards with which to deal,
I'll keep my solid gaze.

Inside Sight

When the arm's curve you see now
retorts, those impossible gold limbs roll.

The corners of substance become like thick air,
a bottom and top, all same and all different.

The line continues with the certainty of wave, no end.
All this in an oval, smooth and fat, shapes balancing.

A bird's mad beak drops an egg into a vase,
but never the movement of falling.

Black curves keep crossing. These are the geese of glory,
pulling the hair of another, forming a hurt-ring.

The Milk

"Go easy with the milk," I said. But before I finished the word milk of the sentence, my head was under. My skirt was soggy. Everything was white. The spoon drifted across my eyebrows. The living room was beginning to turn milky. My mother floated out of the door on the dinner tray. Without any effort, I lifted from the chair. The moon was white, and the sky itself slowly turned from black to gray.

Kitchen of the Sleepless

No one left in this spacious room.
This is the best place to sit.
A kettle's whistle drawn to a close,
soup finished shaking in the bowl of a spoon.
The light has nothing
except a chair to rest on.
Spare the gestures. Nothing to show.

The birds outside on the sill
call their faintest call.
I am still here, my hands empty on the table.
And I lose track of what sleeps,
the stove cracking, breath against the glass,
this room stirring in its own space.

The Way to Spell a Word

However much, however the smile holds, however
much we take with us, a polished pail pulled to our side,
a coin spent yesterday and still gleaming.
We wish what works would win, fully drawn,
the spirit of space bold and unbroken, boat or barge,
apart from the hand, the darkness between the braids,
the white between the fingers; we translate, we swallow
these two words and wait with these, stand, we stand,
the parlors full of glass, the street a row of cars like heavy beads,
a broken hymn and with those, light, a blue ribbon, a shoulder,
a wake from the passing figure, a shadow passing, the nature
of empty, the narrow path on which we walk, a wavering breath.
The sky repeats itself as we pass from this room to the next.

The Grand Table

Whatever is grand, this dish of blue
fruit. This table is clear as my eye
now looking.
Leave it here and you will see that it is still
here tomorrow, cracked and bluer.

The moon looks loose as an old button.
Clouds form against the wind their uneven, held groups.

The fruit turns stone, larger than the sky.
We stand into the beach like needles, losing balance,
too straight to lean without falling.
The table's four legs push deeper toward
water underneath.
An ocean in which no ease is ever found.

Fission

Tonight the moon bears down
on the Mississippi, folds cutting
the yellow underbelly and tossing
marks deep as trenches in the levee.
The river forms its crescent, too,
and curves against this city, a bed
of white lights moving in the dark.

Same place I have always come to, same sound
of water turning, a woman laughing
at the far end of the Moon Walk.
When I turn around, Saint Louis Cathedral looks
even brighter, steeple pinned forever
to that same loosening cloud.

Decatur Street and Governor Nichols, the same corner
where I stood, five years old, with my grandmother.
Wind traveled around us and lifted her hair.
She took my hand and made it into an L,
and we turned left down the block.

The people cross ahead, couples unclasping,
then drifting together there again.
I feel myself passing through—
an idling circle in a long shaft, turning slowly, going out.

III

Arrival

I come to you like the wind
on the high seas, heavy and slight.
My purse is full of luck.
I say you are too serious.
Your heart expands in the immeasurable night.

The land recovers up to the sky,
a memory filters into a darkness
we both know.
The metal cup in your tent spins
on its base, and you tell me the earth
must be speeding up its revolution.

I am finally empty,
iridescent at the edge,
following a cool line to the entrance flap.
You are an unequal scream.
You must watch, if only you would,
because soon the air around your face
will be all you need.

Heliograph

Whether for message or for light,
there's no use.
The sun's undone and repeats its imperceptible
motion, signs flashed not unlike figures in Cubism—
signs across the bay, signs held up
for this night's sinking boat,
one last hand waving from the surface.
What keeps us waiting for the next shift
in shape, surrendered like possums
in a heavy crawl?
That brim of white caught on the lid
of land leaves our eyes wide; we
are without saints—
those who follow us in succession,
canonized and full of white light.

We feed from awkward rays,
held up by their unleashed magnetism,
no magnets, but reflections, signals
we must know the pattern for.
How what flings at our dish-like
corneas, facedown, seems so remote
and blurred, dark wings crossing dark sand.
We take what clues we can, secret
language, wear sharp triangles,
fever under the hold of whatever signifier,
what calls us there.

Acquaintance

I don't know when I heard him last.
He's remembering me, this minute, a red coat and hat.
A curtain comes down like a sheet of ice.
Gray that is not sectional.
A hand pushes over my eyes,
a pursuit closer now to his hold.
First, a lock of hair, then each fingernail.
I'm crossing the street and into his glance.
A singular man, large, if nothing else,
for that moment large in my presence.
My skirt is black, and around my waist,
a belt with a clear ruby.
With each one step of mine, his is twice as long.
I try to disappear.
Into the house, the living room, then a corner.
I wear myself thin.
I look around, the blue rug, the white pitcher
on the end table, the chest near the door.
Then everything, like an early time
that has grown late, everything leaves.
I walk out of the screen door,
down the steps, and onto the sidewalk.

Balthus' Living Room

Forward she lunges, balanced and stretched between
a crawl and a lie—motion awkwardly caught.
Held up by knee and knee, weak hand, and an elbow,
an unnatural way, her back an impossible flat.
Another reclining on the blue chaise longue as if lost in slow sleep
or boredom lounges, her head limp and loose
as a heavy flag. She may go unnoticed and blend in,
for the upholstery's a similar hue to her wrinkled dress
and her arm hides, too, along a curved line.
The girl on the floor pinches at air on a page
of paper, as if holding a tiny shading pencil:
of a cloud, or a figure, or light descending a hill?
Certainly not of the perfect still life, a crystal
bowl of peaches. They loom high, out of sight,
out of interest. Her eyes drift into the floorboards'
hidden darkness. These two are lifeless, linked
somehow by their unmoved modeling, lazy
props for a promised play, peculiar and content.
Minutes spent, a crown of dismal white,
hidden foot there and back there, another, rug-covered.
The silence crosses the room like a gloved hand.
Sleep, a lagging time they've missed, spreads over.

Still Life with Woman

Sometimes she seems
what she cannot seem.
A moss-colored sky
on the fringe of her skirt.
She leaves us head down,
her neck a tiny white pillar
but bending. She does not wear
the last link, like sand,
new, barely a shape in her hand-
held dream, a wishbone,
light on dark, losing itself in the spin.

In Distance

I was lying still in bed. The lamp was on. The fan spun its
wing-shaped shadows around the room. Light came from the
chest of drawers.

How could I be so like someone in a dream, my breath
a water drip,
and in a dream, I tried to catch anyone's attention,
sounds misarranged,
vowels in the throat, vowels in the closet's shelf.
In a dream where nothing made sense—
carrying buckets of water to the bedside.
Shape behind. Shape in front. A train having wings, landing in
the blue brush of a valley. And where was the soft dark of early
evening? Instead, a sun that spread across the lake's weightless
surface.

Far from this house,
I counted whatever movement—lost and then found—distant
leaves shaking, river flowing south, hand waving, dark bone
against white sky. My hand reached for a woman's hair,
stitch finding its way to the next stitch,
movement in the hill's unvarying silence,
a worm still in turned figure, crescent
but waning, a will in the night's unseamed pocket.

Far from this time,
a time unapproached, time caught
against the jawbone's sleep grind.

Far from the distance perceived by a finger
on the pine tree, mark on the knuckle's third line.

Far and near, message prescribed,
light in the sheet, shape in the distance, and here,
all that keeps, unwilling to rise and watch from.

Walking Through

We are speechless tonight, the town a vision
in a squint; the dust blows, the sound on the mark,
on the dot, on the leafless tree. You take the steep
step, the locust resting on its imaginary bark, the snag
in this that hung over the edge, the sag, the snap.
The dogs are fresh to the fields, their little paws are small
and white, the light has lost itself on their fur.
Dawn comes quick, everything that is left, last, the strap
that's ended, the fingers flat. And they have come,
the leashes a knot that ties itself again.

Love Poem

For this, she has taken my hand,
a saturated moon, and called it her own.
The light now shifts the trees.
She must be somewhere now,
walking down a narrow path,
and I with a blue ribbon,
a lamp, walk too.
We are like the sound of water turning,
identical bodies joined cross-like,
and there, beneath, a palm leaf's long stem.

What does she keep in her golden hair-bun?
A set of tools? A hinge? A wooden spool?
She waits for me—I think maybe now,
behind the closet's dark door.
Her breasts fall heavy on the night;
the lake around the back rises even without
a tide, timid, pressing, a heart
pulsing into the earth.

Two Children Are Threatened by a Nightingale

I have no idea why the sky
is yellow where it meets the ground,
why my knife is small, why the man in the suit
on the roof cannot reach the knob.
Why is the gate open?
It is the nightingale who knows.
What is above is made of blue air,
darker toward the heaven.
The arch in the grass could tumble
and spill into a jar. There is myself,
too, who lies on the ground sleeping.
Where have I gone? The nightingale
swallowed my heart while singing last night.
We are without mercy.
The handle on the side of the house
is a tiny plane's propeller.
The man carries a girl in his arms
like a bag of water.
He is about to fly and may spill her.

Blind Swimmer

Those streams you find idling
in your head, unbroken and continuous,
you soften them with definition.
They are too many to define, avenues
of hair, delicate as a swallow.
It's the call of feeling, when everything
is dark, eyes are wide as pools.
It's always night. When a man shuffling down
the street is really the wind,
when a door closing is a clap.
It is never the time to go to sleep.
Touching walls, almost moving them,
measuring every room,
you feel everything around you,
the air in your face, the pages of a book.
You create the story under your fingertips.
The woman at the surface is calling your name,
but only the current
guides you to her.

The Bowl

I am standing at the bottom of my last step.
Low (I am turning now), there's a purple bowl
—a cat's—turned over and something
spilled.

This whole October, these leaves
go slowly down and away.
Nothing next to the bowl, its bowl-shape
turned bottom-up and dull.

Then all is as it was before.
A cat churning lavender water
as hurriedly as a motor.
Whose bowl?
Whose door behind me if not mine?
I am growing small as that light
that sits on the fence nails,
all of the edges disappearing.

This Winter

I am tired of the way the cold comes in,
leaves gone, and the slow finger of a hand
telling me *no*. Let loose the sun's
scattered light, the bird's loud voice.
I am tired of these dreams of running and catching
the smooth air in my hands and the curves of my face.
There's nothing that looks toward shifting
in winter. The waters in Louisiana
do not grow stagnant; the slough behind the cabin
I remember best, its thin layer of algae
a duck now swims across.
I am tired of the woman who comes in my dream
with her head wrapped tight as a baby.
She keeps calling, and around her, the blue light
drifts and rips. She lifts and curves her finger to me.

In the Tone of Waking

Outside, the braided shade of trees
make it difficult to walk.
The birds have found a nesting
in their own driven call,
and the fist falls heavy on the sky. We wake
from an irreversible sleep, slip quietly
in our white gowns down the steep stairs.
Who comes fast in this cold air?
Tight in the mark of dawn's crowd we move,
unreplaced by this moon's make.
Lifeless, unsung, down in the mood's move,
undone, the cross-stitched moon traveling
upward, toward the coastal sound.

Leaving Iowa

We separate in coastal rounds.
We lock our hearts in rapid loss.

With the effort of string, loose
and endless, an inching here

and there, the wind lies down
on our house, a lengthening gray stroke,
hung and motionless.

It is the pairing of split sound
that causes our ear to deepen
with blindfolded failure, and far

between, the black birds seek a kinder existence,
a white expanse moving without edges,
and we are standing, two lines intersecting, just there.

for Bob

The Other Side of Things

It is two o'clock on Sunday.
No word from the first name called, from the whisper
spoken from the inside of a pocket.
The duck loses its feathers in the gray air.
I have a stack of quarters too slick to count. The clouds
resemble small smudges, unclear pictures hesitating
across a clear frame, frame by frame.
What marks the tie is as brief as the race itself; like the smooth surface
of a purse, these things always feel comfortable, white between
white, or the drab hollow of an empty cup. Inside, we forgive
what has been forgotten, bind those things we can't find
with a string, first the finger there to start the knot. The other
side is always a minute in the past.

You Are Waiting

You take the pile that does not worry;
the man leaves his curb.
What delivery has brought him here?
You take what makes the mystery mark,
a dollop of pride pulled up in white socks.
No matter what tune the pilot plays,
he licks the strings of his ordinary violin,
one made of wood, too unknown,
a string loosely wound around the neck.
You have a bright stone, the long stone
that makes the fountain flow, a memory
tied like shoes. You spend the night
inside his pillow, sleep in pride's stolen pocket.
Mercy contracts and falls full, a spent dime
that works its *own* mystery down,
folding a blanket's corner.

October in Virginia

It is with ease that we break free,
ride our saddles thin as ice; we spin
in the moment's red glaze, an avenue wide
and green. You know what blames this truth,
sideways like a deer's clear vision.
The rain has stopped, the length
of a minute lengthens like a thin strand of yarn
from a blanket. It is cold as ever.
The robins have little to do but shiver.
The windows of the room have all but disappeared.
Branches break; bones on the face caught,
cupped, canned in what seems an hour.
Her body loosens, and the wind, gray and odd,
wraps around this small house.

In the morning, bleached sky over an unmoving
pond, a puddle in the brain. The cat leaps
from a steel tube and lands, solid and still.
Underneath it all, the ground must leak a slow leak.

The Drive

It's time the fireflies live long,
leap into the field's palm;
a cold clasp on the locket of the lip,
like the highway's strip of light never ending,
slim and blurred across the view, I too
become a kind of edge, the bitten hold.

It's time the ducks waste their white wings,
move along in the lagoon, brave
and without what once held them to be white.

It's time there is light on this wide expanse;
the face's frequent expression, telling
the hand's off-hand remark, surfacing,
the wheel catching what sound now held there.

It's time this dark space separates what true inches
there are, odd, even, or split; shoulder to shoulder,
edge to edge, the creek rises, a black line outside the window.